Loving Mum

Mindfulness
Adult Coloring Book

Thank you for your purchase and we hope you enjoy this book.

If you do enjoy this book , please take the time, to visit Amazon.com and leave a review as this helps others find this book.

I am grounded in this present moment.

I breath in calmness, I breath out tension

My mind is clear, my heart is open

I am a beacon of peace and serenity

I release worries and embrace tranquility

Each breath I take brings me closer to
inner peace

I am grateful for the beauty of this moment

I am mindful of the beauty around me

I let go of what I cannot control

I am connected to the energy of the universe

I trust the journey, even when I do not understand it

I am centred, I am present, I am here

I am aware of my thoughts, but I am not defined by them

I am a vessel of love and kindness

I am the master of my thoughts and emotions

I am open to the wisdom that arises within me

I am at peace with my past, present
and future

I am a channel for positivity and harmony

I am a source of calm in any situation

I am a magnet for positive energy

I am gentle with myself and others

I trust the timing of my life's journey

I am a beacon of light in the world

I am present, I am aware, I am alive

I am attuned to the rhythm of life

I am a vessel of compassion and understanding

I am grateful for the lessons that
challenges bring

Thank you once again for purchasing this book. I hope it has been fulfilling.

If you enjoyed this book, please take a few moments to leave a review on Amazon.com as this helps others find this book.

If you enjoyed this book, check out Jason's best seller Quiet Mind, available on Amazon.com

Sample Images

Mindfulness

Quiet Mind

Adult Coloring Book